ACHIEVE LEVEL 4

ENGLISH

By **Gill Matthews**
with additional material from
Alison Clarke, Laura Collins and **Richard Cooper**

RISING ★ STARS

PLEASE NOTE: THIS BOOK MAY NOT BE PHOTOCOPIED OR REPRODUCED AND WE APPRECIATE YOUR HELP IN PROTECTING OUR COPYRIGHT.

Rising Stars UK Ltd., 76 Farnaby Road, Bromley, BR1 4BH
www.risingstars-uk.com

Every effort has been made to trace copyright holders and obtain their permission for the use of copyright material. The authors and publishers will gladly receive information enabling them to rectify any error or omission in subsequent editions.

All facts are correct at time of going to press.

Published 2003
New edition 2003
Reprinted 2004 twice
This new colour edition 2005

Text, design and layout © Rising Stars UK Ltd.
Educational Consultants: Alison Clarke and Angie Cooper

Cover design: Burville Riley

Design: Techset Composition Limited

Illustrations: Burville Riley, Beehive Illustration (Theresa Tibbetts), Graham-Cameron Illustration (Anthony Maher and Leighton Noyes)

Cover illustration: Beehive Illustration (Theresa Tibbetts)

All rights reserved. No part of this publication may be reproduced, stored in a retrieval system, or transmitted in any form by any means, electronic, mechanical, photocopying, recording or otherwise without the prior permission of Rising Stars UK Ltd.

British Library Cataloguing in Publication Data
A CIP record for this book is available from the British Library.

ISBN 1-905056-02-8

Printed by Craft Print International Ltd, Singapore

Acknowledgements
p58–59, from *Smile!* by Geraldine McCaughrean (OUP, 2004) © Geraldine McCaughrean 2004. Published and used with the permission of Oxford University Press.
p60, Ian McMillan "Ten things found in a wizard's pocket" and "Counting the stars" © 2001 from *The Very Best of Ian McMillan* © Ian McMillan. Published and used with the permission of Macmillan Children's Books.

Contents

How to use this book	4
Achieve Level 4 English – Objectives	6
The National Tests	7
Test tips and techniques	9
Writing non-ficton	10
Writing fiction	24
Grammar	36
Punctuation	43
Vocabulary	47
Spelling	49
Reviewing your work	53
Reading comprehension	54
Handwriting	61
Answers	62

How to use this book

WRITING NON-FICTION

1) Definition – This section explains the genre and provides examples of this text type.

2) Self assessment – Colour in the face that best describes your understanding of this concept.

3) Text plan – Each type of writing is explained in a step-by-step way to help you plan. Planning is very important when writing fiction and non-fiction and these charts will help you plan properly.

This icon indicates the section is a *teaching* section.

4) Language features – This section explains the language features used for this type of text, including examples.

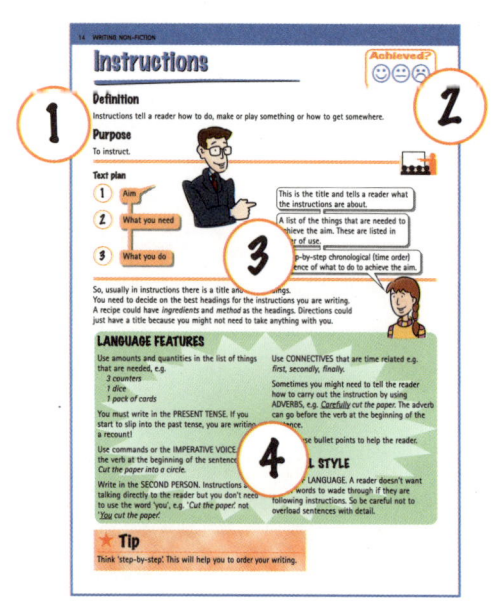

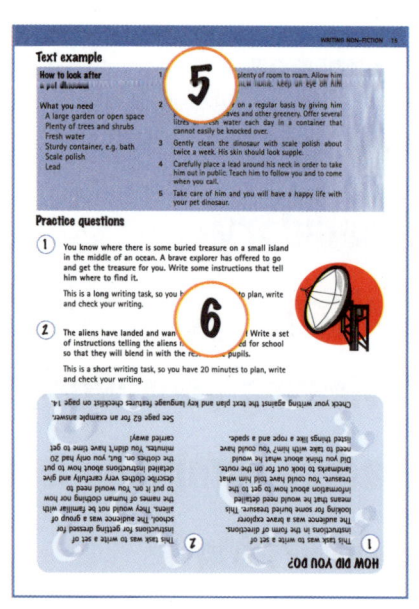

5) Text example – This gives you an example of a well-written piece of text that follows the text plan and contains the key language features.

6) Practice questions – This is where you do the work! Try answering the questions by using the text plan and by referring to the key language features. Compare it against the written example – is your answer good enough for a Level 4?

WRITING FICTION

This section takes you through the key elements of fiction writing:

Definition – This section explains the genre and provides examples of this text type.

Structure – This section provides a model structure for your narrative including examples.

Language Features – This section gives you all you need to know about the type of language used in this text type.

Tips – The tips give you ideas and hints to improve your work and get the best marks.

Practice Questions – These give you the chance to practise your skills.

Reading comprehension

1. Text example – This gives you a typical example of a piece of text that you might find in your SATs.

2. Questions – The text is followed by a number of questions relating to the text. There are 1-, 2- and 3-mark questions so remember to read between the lines.

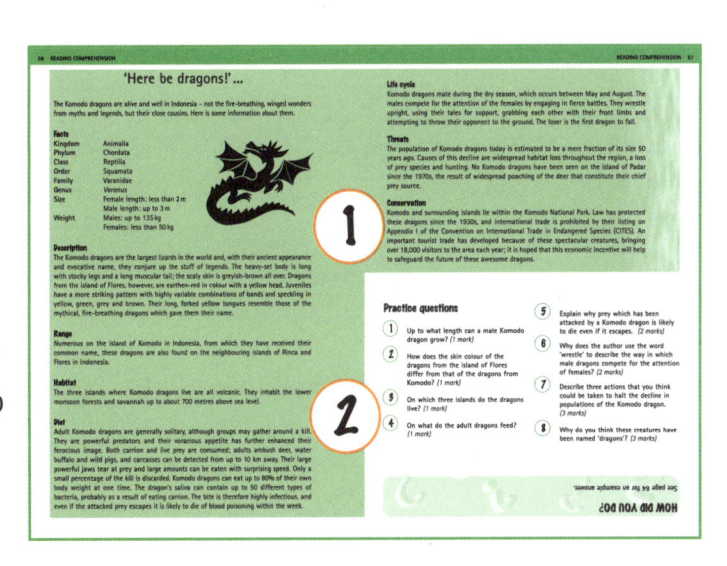

In addition you will find over 100 clear tips and facts to help you with:

★ grammar ★ spelling ★ punctuation ★ vocabulary ★ handwriting

If you use this guidance to help you prepare for your test, you will have a great chance of achieving a Level 4!

Achieve Level 4 English – Objectives

This chart allows you to see which objectives in the National Literacy Strategy have been covered and which are to be completed.

We have matched the objectives with pages of Achieve Level 4 so you can monitor progress.

When children have indicated 'achievement', you can encourage them to tick the box or highlight that row in this table. That way, you and your class know what has been achieved and what is still to be covered.

> Yr = Year
> T = Text level
> W = Word level
> S = Sentence level

Page no.	Title	Objective	Achieved? (tick)
12-13	Recount	Yr 5 Term 1 T24	
14-15	Instructions	Yr 5 Term 1 T25	
16-17	Non-chronological report	Yr 5 Term 2 T22 Yr 6 Term 1 T17	
18-19	Explanation	Yr 5 Term 2 T22	
20-21	Persuasion	Yr 5 Term 3 T19	
22-23	Balanced argument	Yr 6 Term 2 T18, T19	
24-35	Writing fiction	Yr 4 Term 1 T1, T2, T3, T4, T9, T10; Term 2 T1, T2, T3, T4, T8, T10, T13; Term 3 T1, T3, T11, T13 Yr 5 Term 1 T1, T2, T3, T11; Term 2 T1, T9, T11, T13 Yr 6 Term 1 T6, T7	
36-42	Grammar	Yr 4 Term 1 S1, S5, T15; Term 2 S2, S3, S4; Term 3 S2, S3, S4	
43-46	Punctuation	Yr 5 Term 1 S3, S5, S6, S7, S8; Term 2 S8, S9; Term 3 S4, S5, S6, S7 Yr 6 Term 1 S4, S5; Term 2 S3, S4, S5	
47-48	Vocabulary	Yr 4 Term 1 S4; Term 2 W9, S1 Yr 5 Term 1 W7, W10	
49-52	Spelling	Yr 4 Term 1 W3, W7, W8; Term 2 W4 Yr 5 Term 1 W1, W2, W3, W5; Term 2 W1, W2, W3, W4; Term 3 W1, W2, W3, W4, W5, W6 Yr 6 Term 1 W1, W2, W3, W4	
53	Reviewing your work	Yr 5 Term 2 T13, T24, S1, S2, S3 Yr 6 Term 3 S1	
54-59	Reading comprehension	Yr 4 Term 1 T1, T2, T16, T17, T18, T19; Term 2 T1, T2, T3, T4, T5, T17 Yr 5 Term 1 T3, T22; Term 2 T1, T8, T9, T10, T15, T16; Term 3 T2 Yr 6 Term 1 T3	
61	Handwriting	Yr 4 Term 3 W13, W14	

The National Tests

Key facts

★ The Key Stage 2 National Tests (or SATs) take place in the middle of May in Year 6. You will be tested on Maths, English and Science.

★ The tests take place in your school but will be promptly sent away to be marked by examiners – not your teacher!

★ You will usually get your results in July, two months after you take the tests.

★ Individual test scores are not made public. However, a school's combined scores are published in what are commonly known as league tables.

The English National Tests

You will take four tests in English. These are designed to test your Reading, Writing and Spelling. Your handwriting will be assessed through the Writing Test.

The Writing Test

There are two Writing Tasks - one shorter (about 20 minutes) and one longer task (about 45 minutes). Remember to keep your handwriting neat for these tasks.

The Short Writing Task is 20 minutes long. You should plan very briefly using the given prompts in no longer than 2–3 minutes. Remember that you only have 20 minutes in total, but still need to include a 1-minute check at the end.

The Long Writing Task is 45 minutes long. You should aim for 10 minutes planning at the most. You must use the given plan and not any other separate paper or planner. However, these planning sheets will not be marked. Try your best to maximise the time you have for writing and ALWAYS spend 3–5 minutes re-reading and checking.

Where to go to get help

Pages 10 to 35 are designed to help you succeed in the Writing Tests, and include information about writing fiction and non-fiction.

Pages 36 to 52 will help you to give 'voice' to your writing, sharpen up your punctuation and improve your grammar.

Page 61 gives you advice on how to improve your handwriting, which is marked through the Long Writing Task only.

The Reading Test

There is one test to assess your reading comprehension. It will last about 1 hour. In this test you will be given a series of texts and an answer paper. You will be allowed to use the texts to answer the questions, so you won't need to memorise them. You should refer to the texts closely while you are answering.

Where to go to get help
Pages 54 to 59 give you advice on how to answer reading comprehension questions, which will help with the Reading Test.

The Spelling Test

There is one 15-minute Spelling Test. Your teacher will read a passage (or play a CD with someone else reading the passage). You will have to write the words to complete the passage.

Where to go to get help
Pages 49 to 52 give you practice in spelling, including a list of key words to learn before your test.

Don't forget!

1. There is one Long Writing Task and one Short Writing Task.

2. Handwriting will only be assessed in the Long Writing Task – there is no separate handwriting test.

3. In the Reading Test, refer to the text to find your answers.

Test tips and techniques

Before SATs

- Reading will help you to be a better writer, so read as much as you can. Read as a writer and write as a reader. In other words, think about the writer when you read – what did they mean? And think about the reader when you write – how do I want them to feel?
- Have you got a sharp pencil, clean rubber, ruler and working pen? Gather them together ready to take to school.
- Get a good night's sleep the night before. Go to bed at a reasonable time – not too early, not too late. Don't worry – worrying won't change anything.
- Food helps you to think and concentrate. Try to have some cereal and fruit for breakfast, every morning before your tests.
- Leave the house on time. You don't want to be late and in a panic!

The National Tests

Writing

- Before you start, look carefully at each of the tasks. Remember "Read the question and then read it again." Look for **why** you are writing and **who** the reader is. Think about the organisation, content and style that you will use.
- Think, and then make notes on the planning sheet. You need to make notes about the content and organisation of your writing. Also, if you think of words and phrases that you believe will work, write them down too. Don't take any more than 10 minutes to plan.
- Refer to your plan when you are writing.
- Remember that your handwriting is being looked at in the longer writing task. If you make a mistake, either put a neat line through it – one line, not a huge scribble – or rub it out.
- Make sure you leave some checking time at the end of the task. Things to check:
  – Read your writing: does it make sense?
  – Are your paragraphs clear?
  – Are there any words you can improve?
  – Do your spellings look right?
  – Have you got the basics right and used full stops, capital letters, sentences?

Reading

- Read the title of the reading booklet. What is it about? Now read through the booklet slowly and carefully. You are given time to do this in the test so make the most of it. Re-read anything that you don't understand the first time. Use a pencil to highlight key words.
- The first few questions in the booklet will be 1-mark questions. They may appear easy, but don't rush them because these are your 'bread and butter' marks.
- Look to see how many marks a question is worth. The 2- and 3-mark questions will require you to answer in more depth. A 3-mark question usually requires an in-depth answer OR three separate points. Remember to read between the lines. Always back up your opinions with reasons from the text. If you say something is 'because', then say why.
- After 20 minutes you should be roughly halfway through.
- You should allow yourself 5 minutes at the end to read through your answers, spot any mistakes and re-visit any questions you were stuck on first time around.
- Never leave a multiple choice question. You might get lucky, even if you guess!

WRITING NON-FICTION

Non-fiction texts give you information about something or someone. They also give you facts and, sometimes, opinions.

Type of non-fiction	Definition	Where you might read an example
Recount	A recount tells you about something that has happened in the past. It may include personal opinions and comments.	Letters, diaries, newspaper articles and news reports.
Instructions	Instructions tell you how to do something in a step-by step way.	Instructions for board games, building models, recipes, directions, how to repair something, etc.
Non-chronological report	Non-chronological reports give facts about a subject.	Encyclopedias, information books, posters and leaflets, travel guides, etc.
Explanation	Explanations tell the reader how or why things happen, or how and why something works.	Leaflets, posters, manuals, letters, diagrams and information books.
Persuasion	Persuasive writing will try to influence the way someone thinks about a person or subject.	Advertising posters, articles, leaflets and SPAM email.
Balanced argument/ Discussion	Both viewpoints are given and the readers are left to make up their own mind.	Newspaper articles, newspaper letter pages, magazines, information leaflets and posters.

KEY FACTS - Writing Non-fiction

To be a solid Level 4 in your non-fiction writing you need to:

- Know the purpose and the audience you are writing for
- Use the correct text structure and language features
- Organise your writing into paragraphs
- Use the correct connectives
- Vary your sentence types

Over to you!

1. Work through each section and don't rush.
2. Learn the purpose of the text type.
3. Make sure you understand the way it is organised and what the key language features are.
4. Have a go at the practice questions.

The practice questions

Look at the PURPOSE of the piece of writing you are being asked to do. This is the big clue that tells you which text type to write. The question might say "Write a letter that gives information about..." Straight away, this tells you that you will be writing a non-chronological report. It might say "Write a letter to persuade someone to..." This tells you that you will be writing a persuasive text. Get the idea?

Look at the AUDIENCE for your writing. This is the clue that tells you what kind of language to include. The question might say "Write a letter to your mum and dad". This tells you that you will be using informal language because you know your audience. It might say "Write a report for the local museum". This tells you that you will be using formal, polite language because you don't know your audience.

Once you have decided on the text type, plan, write and check your writing.

THINK ABOUT:

- **Text structure** – Is it well organised? Have you used paragraphs?
- **Language features** and **text type** – Have you used some of the key language features? Have you used a variety of the right sort of connectives? Is it in the right tense?
- **Language and audience** – Are the words and phrases that you've used right for the audience?

THE END

When you have worked through a section, you could make a poster that sums up the:

- purpose
- text structure
- key language features

Keep this to remind yourself quickly about these three important things.

Recount

Achieved?

Definition

A recount is a piece of writing that gives information about something that has happened in the past. A recount should include personal feelings and comment.

Purpose

To retell an event or events.

Text plan

1. Introduction
2. Events
3. Summary

- *When* and *where* it happened.
- *Who* was involved.
- *What* happened in chronological (time) order.
- *Why* it happened.
- *How* someone felt about it.

Look at the words in *italics*. You could use these as headings to help you plan a recount. Think about organising your recount into three paragraphs.

LANGUAGE FEATURES

Events in a recount have already happened, so use verbs in the PAST TENSE e.g. *We rode to the park.* not *We ride to the park.*

If you are in the recount, use the FIRST PERSON *I*, *we*, *us*. e.g. *We went to see the new Harry Potter film.*

If you are writing about someone else, use the THIRD PERSON *he*, *she*, *they*. e.g. *He scored the winning goal.*

TYPICAL STYLE

Recounts can be INFORMAL if you know the audience or FORMAL if you don't.

★ Tip

Recounts can be in the form of a letter, diary entry, biography, autobiography, newsletter article, sports report and news report. Remember to think about the **purpose** of the text!

Text example

Our school play

Last Tuesday evening an audience of proud parents crowded into the school hall. They were there to watch the first performance of this year's school play. The play, 'The First Letter,' was written by Y6 teacher Miss Reid.

First, the audience was entertained by the school orchestra. They played some tunes and soon many of the parents were singing along. Next, the play started. It was an exciting first half with Robert Higgs in the lead role. Everyone agreed that he was fantastic as the cunning magician. Then it was time for the interval. Drinks and biscuits were served by some of the parents. After a 20 minute break, the play restarted. The audience was on the edge of their seats until the last moment.

Finally Mrs Jones, the headteacher, stood up to thank everyone. "It has been a great success," she said. The audience clapped loudly as Molly Dodd, the youngest pupil in the school, presented Miss Reid with some flowers. As one parent said: "It was a wonderful evening. I'm really glad I came."

Practice questions

1 You have recently been on a school trip. Write an article for the school newsletter that tells parents about what happened on the trip.

This is a **long** writing task, so you have 45 minutes to plan, write and check your writing.

2
> Little Miss Muffet
> Sat on a tuffet
> Eating her curds and whey.
> There came a big spider
> That sat down beside her
> And frightened Miss Muffet away!

Not a pleasant day for Miss Muffet! Write the spider's diary entry for the day.

This is a **short** writing task, so you have 20 minutes to plan, write and check your writing.

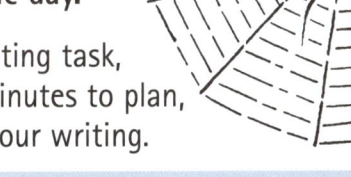

HOW DID YOU DO?

1 This task was to write a recount in the form of an article for the school newsletter. The audience was the parents who read the newsletter. This means that it should be quite a formal piece of writing but with some interesting, and perhaps funny, information. It could be a mix of first and third person. You will need to have explained who people in the article are because the parents won't know the names of everyone in the school. Look back at the text example to see how this was done.

2 This task was to write a diary entry by the spider in the nursery rhyme. Usually people keep diaries just for themselves – not for the whole world to read. So, the audience was the spider himself. This means that it should have been informal, with brief language.

Check your writing against the text plan and key language features checklist on page 12.

Instructions

Definition
Instructions tell a reader how to do, make or play something or how to get somewhere.

Purpose
To instruct.

Text plan

1. Aim
2. What you need
3. What you do

- This is the title and tells a reader what the instructions are about.
- A list of the things that are needed to achieve the aim. These are listed in order of use.
- A step-by-step chronological (time order) sequence of what to do to achieve the aim.

So, usually in instructions there is a title and two headings.
You need to decide on the best headings for the instructions you are writing.
A recipe could have *ingredients* and *method* as the headings. Directions could just have a title because you might not need to take anything with you.

LANGUAGE FEATURES

Use amounts and quantities in the list of things that are needed, e.g.
 3 counters
 1 dice
 1 pack of cards

You must write in the PRESENT TENSE. If you start to slip into the past tense, you are writing a recount!

Use commands or the IMPERATIVE VOICE. Put the verb at the beginning of the sentence, e.g. *Cut the paper into a circle.*

Write in the SECOND PERSON. Instructions are talking directly to the reader but you don't need to use the word 'you', e.g. '*Cut the paper.*' not '*You cut the paper.*'

Use CONNECTIVES that are time related e.g. *first, secondly, finally.*

Sometimes you might need to tell the reader how to carry out the instruction by using ADVERBS, e.g. *Carefully* cut the paper. The adverb can go before the verb at the beginning of the sentence.

You can use bullet points to help the reader.

TYPICAL STYLE

Use BRIEF LANGUAGE. A reader doesn't want lots of words to wade through if they are following instructions. So be careful not to overload sentences with detail.

★ Tip
Think 'step-by-step'. This will help you to order your writing.

WRITING NON-FICTION

Text example

How to look after a pet dinosaur

What you need
- A large garden or open space
- Plenty of trees and shrubs
- Fresh water
- Sturdy container, e.g. bath
- Scale polish
- Lead

1. Your dinosaur needs plenty of room to roam. Allow him time to explore his new home. Keep an eye on him from a distance.
2. Feed your dinosaur on a regular basis by giving him plenty of fresh leaves and other greenery. Offer several litres of fresh water each day in a container that cannot easily be knocked over.
3. Gently clean the dinosaur with scale polish about twice a week. His skin should look supple.
4. Carefully place a lead around his neck in order to take him out in public. Teach him to follow you and to come when you call.
5. Take care of him and you will have a happy life with your pet dinosaur.

Practice questions

1 You know where there is some buried treasure on a small island in the middle of an ocean. A brave explorer has offered to go and get the treasure for you. Write some instructions that tell him where to find it.

This is a **long** writing task, so you have 45 minutes to plan, write and check your writing.

2 The aliens have landed and want to come to school! Write a set of instructions telling the aliens how to get dressed for school so that they will blend in with the rest of the pupils.

This is a **short** writing task, so you have 20 minutes to plan, write and check your writing.

How did you do?

1 This task was to write a set of instructions in the form of directions. The audience was a brave explorer looking for some buried treasure. This means that he would need detailed information about how to get to the treasure. You could have told him what landmarks to look out for on the route. Did you think about what he would need to take with him? You could have listed things like a rope and a spade.

2 This task was to write a set of instructions for getting dressed for school. The audience was a group of aliens. They would not be familiar with the names of human clothing nor how to put it on. You would need to describe clothes very carefully and give detailed instructions about how to put the clothes on. But, you only had 20 minutes. You didn't have time to get carried away!

See page 62 for an example answer.

Check your writing against the text plan and key language features checklist on page 14.

Non-chronological report

Achieved?

Definition
Non-chronological reports give a reader information about something or somewhere. They are usually about a group of things, e.g. dinosaurs, not one thing in particular, e.g. Dilly the dinosaur. Facts about the subject are organised into paragraphs.

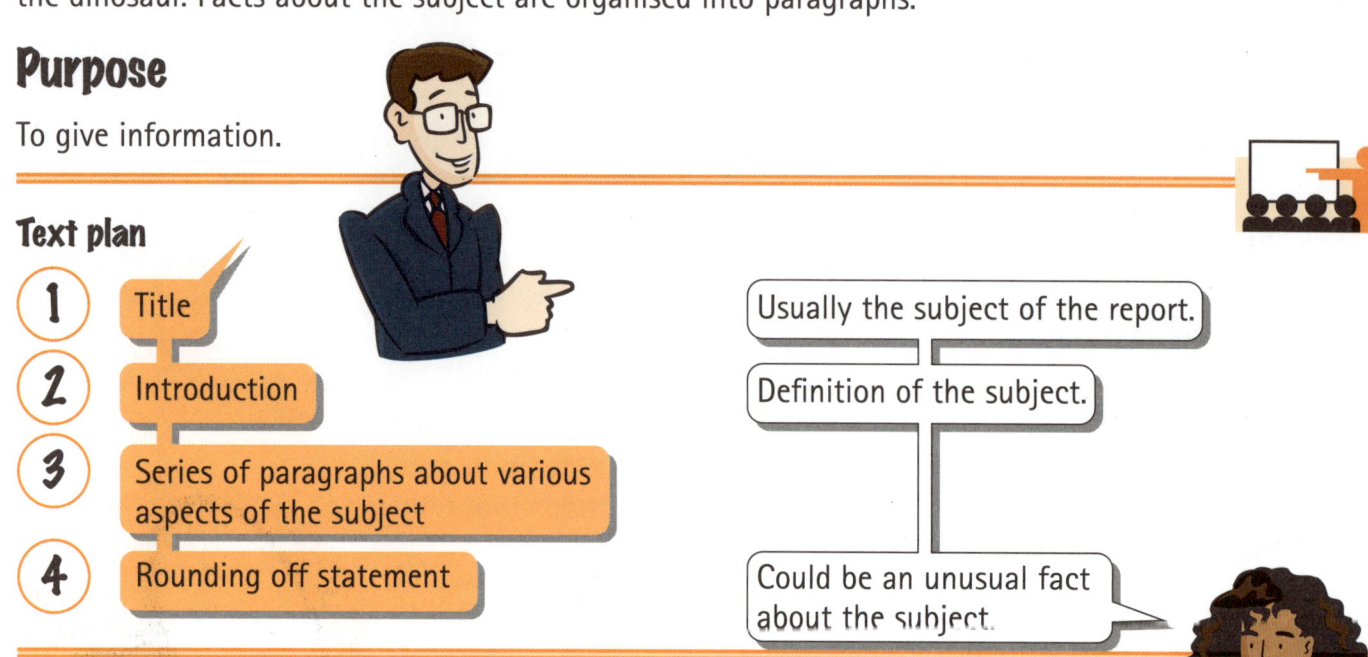

Purpose
To give information.

Text plan
1. Title — Usually the subject of the report.
2. Introduction — Definition of the subject.
3. Series of paragraphs about various aspects of the subject
4. Rounding off statement — Could be an unusual fact about the subject.

Paragraphs are the key to writing non-chronological reports. Try to use at least two paragraphs after the introduction and before the rounding off statement.
Decide what each paragraph is going to be about and only have that information in there.

LANGUAGE FEATURES

Use the PRESENT TENSE if the subject still exists, e.g. *Crocoraffes have scaly skin*. Write in the PAST TENSE if the subject does not still exist, e.g. *Dinosaurs had scaly skin*.

Use TECHNICAL VOCABULARY (language about the subject), e.g. *Crocoraffes are omnivores*.

Use ADJECTIVES to give more information about a fact, e.g. *They also have very sharp teeth and strong jaws.*

TYPICAL STYLE

Use an IMPERSONAL VOICE. Don't say what you think or give your opinions. So, don't write *Crocoraffes are large scary animals* because using the word 'scary' gives your opinion away. You could write *Crocoraffes are large animals* because then you are just stating the facts.

★ Tip
Reports can be in the form of letters, encyclopedia entries, information posters or leaflets, as well as a straightforward piece of writing. A non-chronological report on a school might include headings such as: Number of pupils; After school clubs; Location.

WRITING NON-FICTION

Text example

Crocoraffes

Crocoraffes are large animals. They can breathe and eat, both in and out of water. They were discovered on April 1st 2000 by the explorer Sir Humbert Bumbert whilst he was trekking through dense jungle.

Crocoraffes are about the size of a large horse. They have scaly skin that has a slightly mottled effect. They have long necks, which they use to reach up into the highest branches for leaves. They also have very sharp teeth and strong jaws in order to catch their prey when swimming underwater. The animal's broad muscular legs push it quickly through the water.

Crocoraffes are omnivores. This means that they eat both leaves and meat. They are attracted by the tender new shoots of the honey tree and can often cause considerable damage to these trees. In the water, crocoraffes will catch and eat up to fifty large fish in a day.

The jungles of South America appear to be the only place where crocoraffes can be found. They keep to the thickest part of the jungle that is rarely, if ever, visited by man. They make large nests from jungle creepers and line them with mud from the river bank. This then hardens to create a sturdy home for a pair of crocoraffes and their offspring.

They can live for as long as forty to fifty years and mate for life. During this partnership a couple can produce as many as a hundred offspring, known as crocoraffettes.

Practice questions

1 Sir Humbert Bumbert has found another rare animal on his travels. He has brought it back to display in his own zoo. Write a leaflet that will be on display outside the animal's enclosure at the zoo.

This is a long writing task, so you have 45 minutes to plan, write and check your writing.

2 Astronauts have discovered a new planet. Write a short letter from one astronaut to his children telling them what the planet is like.

This is a short writing task, so you have 20 minutes to plan, write and check your writing.

HOW DID YOU DO?

1 This task was to write a report in the form of a leaflet. The leaflet will be on display at a zoo, so the audience would be the general public. This means that you need to write in a formal style. You should have introduced and defined the animal, then written another two or three paragraphs. Each paragraph should be about a particular aspect of the animal. You should not have included very much about the discovery of the animal, otherwise it will turn into a recount before your very eyes!

2 This task was to write a report in the form of a brief letter. The audience was the astronaut's children so you could have used a chatty, informal style. But, you should still have sorted the facts into paragraphs. The paragraphs could have been about what the planet looks like, what the aliens who live there do and what is grown on the planet.

See page 62 for an example answer.

Check your writing against the text plan and key language features checklist on page 16.

Explanation

Definition

An explanation tells the reader how or why something works or happens. It can be about natural things, e.g. *why volcanoes erupt*, or about mechanical things, e.g. *how a radio works*.

Purpose

To explain.

Text plan

1. Title — Tells the reader what the explanation is about. Often contains *how* or *why*.
2. Introduction — Definition of the subject of the explanation.
3. Paragraph that describes the parts of the subject or the appearance
4. Paragraph that explains how or why, usually in time order if explaining a process
5. Rounding off paragraph — Could include where the subject can be found or what it is used for.

LANGUAGE FEATURES

Write in the PRESENT TENSE if the subject is still around, e.g. *Robodog <u>is</u> a robotic dog.* Write in the past tense if it existed in the past, e.g. *Dodos <u>were</u> birds.*

Use TIME CONNECTIVES to show the order in which things happen, e.g. *first, next, then, when, once.*

Use CAUSE AND EFFECT CONNECTIVES to show how one thing makes something else happen, e.g. *as, so that, in order to, because.*

Use TECHNICAL VOCABULARY (language about the subject), e.g. *Robodog uses microchips to react to movement and sound.*

TYPICAL STYLE

The PASSIVE VOICE, e.g. *Robodog was developed in Japan in great secrecy* makes an explanation more formal. Don't use it too much because you need variety in your writing.

★ Tip

Explanations can be in the form of letters, diagrams, information leaflets, encyclopedia entries and posters.

Text example

How Robodog works

Robodog is a robotic dog that can be programmed to meet the needs of any owner. They are available in many shops and on the Internet. Robodog owners include the Beckhams, Eminem and, it is believed, the Queen.

The dog looks very much like any normal dog. It is about the size of a poodle and weighs 2kg. Its head is rather angular, with a wet black nose, pointed ears and large brown eyes. Robodog has stocky legs and a short tail that wags rapidly from side to side. The body of the dog is warm to the touch and covered in a material that feels very realistic.

Robodog uses microchips to react to movement and sound. In order to train Robodog to recognise its name, the owner speaks the dog's name three times into the microphone positioned in the left ear. This means that whenever Robodog hears its name it will move towards the source of the sound. Robodog is also able to follow a moving object. When a ball or stick is thrown, Robodog will fetch it. The dog also responds to tone of voice. A cross voice makes its ears droop. A praising voice makes its tail wag even faster and causes it to jump around.

Robodog was developed in Japan in great secrecy. It is thought that scientists are now working on Robocat and Robomouse.

Practice questions

1) You have invented a machine that does your homework for you. Write an article for an inventors' magazine explaining what it does and how it works.

This is a **long** writing task, so you have 45 minutes to plan, write and check your writing.

2) Wayne has come to school without his football kit. Write a note to the teacher from his mum that explains why this has happened.

This is a **short** writing task, so you have 20 minutes to plan, write and check your writing.

HOW DID YOU DO?

1) This task was to write an explanation in the form of a magazine article. The audience would be the readers of the magazine. This means that you should have written in a formal style. Check that you have written in the present tense. If you wrote in the past tense about how you invented the machine, then it has turned into a recount. If you wrote telling the readers how to work the machine themselves, it's turned into instructions!

2) This task was to write an explanation in the form of a note. The audience is the teacher. Chances are that Wayne's mum knows the teacher. This means that the note will be fairly informal but polite. You should have used some cause and effect connectives and probably some time connectives.

See page 62 for an example answer.

Check your writing against the text plan and key language features checklist on page 18.

Persuasion

Definition
A persuasive text tries to make the reader think, do or buy something.

Purpose
To persuade.

Text plan
1. Identify the point of the text
2. Reasons to support the point, organised into paragraphs
3. Summary of the key reasons

LANGUAGE FEATURES

Usually PRESENT TENSE but could move into past or future, depending on the point being made.

Support the reasons with EVIDENCE. This could be numbers and statistics, facts or quotes.

Appeal to your readers emotions by using EMOTIVE LANGUAGE. Make them think about what you are saying and themselves, e.g. *It all costs money and who pays for it? Your readers do!*

Use LOGICAL CONNECTIVES to reason with the reader, e.g. *therefore, consequently, furthermore, so, thus.*

TYPICAL STYLE

Use the PASSIVE VOICE if you don't want to say where you are getting your evidence from, e.g. *it is thought that, it is believed.*

★ Tip

Persuasive texts can be in virtually any form. They can be letters, adverts, posters, leaflets, newspaper and magazine articles. Remember to think about the **purpose** of the text!

Text example

Dear Mr Jones,

I am writing to complain about the quality of the school dinners on offer recently at St Starvin's Primary School.

There have been no fresh fruit or vegetables on offer for the last two weeks. Also the chips and nuggets are always very greasy and unappetising. The standard of desserts is also poor – we have had prunes and semolina every day for a month.

As a result of this a number of Year 6 pupils have refused to eat their lunch and have been tired and unable to concentrate in the afternoon. Our National Tests begin in May and many of us are very concerned that our results will suffer!

Although a small number of pupils do enjoy your fried food, the majority of us are keen to maintain a balanced diet and lead a healthy lifestyle.

Could you please provide us with suggestions for alternative menus? A group of us would be happy to help with this as we have many ideas ourselves.

I look forward to hearing from you.

Yours sincerely

Em T. Tum, Class 6D

Practice questions

1 You are a keen skater but there is nowhere for you to skate safely in your town. Write a letter to the paper complaining about the situation. Write a conclusion summarising your opinion.

This is a **long** writing task, so you have 45 minutes to plan, write and check your writing.

2 Your school is holding a fundraising event. Write an advert for the event that will be displayed in local shop windows.

This is a **short** writing task, so you have 20 minutes to plan, write and check your writing.

HOW DID YOU DO?

1 This task was to write a persuasive text in the form of a letter. The audience is the readers of the newspaper. This means that it should be a formal piece of writing. You need to have thought carefully about your point of view and the reasons you give to support it. Your letter should be organised in paragraphs. In the conclusion, repeat your main points briefly.

2 This task was to write a persuasive text in the form of an advert. The audience is the local public. This means that it should be fairly formal and give key information, e.g. what the event is, when and where it is taking place and what the attractions are. You should have used language to attract the readers to the event.

See page 62 for an example answer.

Check your writing against the text plan and key language features checklist on page 20.

Balanced argument

Definition

An argument gives the reader information about an issue from different points of view, then leaves the reader to make up their mind about how they feel about the issue.

Purpose

To present a balanced argument.

Structure

1. **Title** — Often in the form of a question.
2. **Opening paragraph** — Statement of the issue and a preview of the main arguments.
3. **Points to support the issue** — Arguments for and supporting evidence.
4. **Points against the issue** — Arguments against and supporting evidence. (You could also use argument/counter argument, one point at a time.)
5. **Recommendation** — A summary and conclusion.

LANGUAGE FEATURES

Can be in the PRESENT TENSE or the PAST TENSE, depending on the issue.

Use LOGICAL CONNECTIVES to help you organise your argument, e.g. *therefore, consequently, so.*

Use connectives that show the OPPOSITE view, e.g. *but, however, nevertheless.*

Use a CONNECTIVE in the final paragraph to show that you are SUMMING UP, e.g. *in conclusion, to summarise, as a result, finally.*

Support the reasons with EVIDENCE. This could be numbers and statistics, facts or quotes.

TYPICAL STYLE

Use an IMPERSONAL STYLE. Don't say what you think. Say what other people think.

Use the PASSIVE VOICE, particularly if you don't want to say where you are getting your evidence from, e.g. *it is thought that, it is believed.*

★ Tip

Arguments can be in the form of information leaflets, newspaper and magazine articles. Remember to back up your ideas with evidence.

Text example

Do school children have too many tests?

Primary school children have more tests now than ever before. All children take tests in Y2 and Y6. Some schools also test the children at the end of every year. Parents, teachers and children are beginning to ask whether this is helping children to learn or just testing their memory. It could also be said that the tests are really testing the teachers' ability to teach.

Some people argue that tests are a good thing. They give schools a good idea of what the children have learned and what more they need to learn. They also give parents and children an idea of how the child is progressing. Children who do well in tests will feel good about themselves and continue to work hard.

However, others say that tests put too much pressure on children and that they can become upset and worried. Also, they question whether the tests need to be so frequent. A spokesperson for Parents Against Tests – PAT – said recently, 'Our children are not being taught what they need to know to get on in life. They are being taught how to take tests.'

To summarise, there is clearly plenty to discuss and consider about the issue. The key point is to put the children first.

Practice questions

1
*Humpty Dumpty sat on a wall
Humpty Dumpty had a great fall
All the King's horses and all the King's men
Couldn't put Humpty together again.*

But why did Humpty fall? Was someone else involved? Write the TV news report that presents both sides of this case.

This is a **long** writing task, so you have 45 minutes to plan, write and check your writing.

2
Did he fall or was he pushed? The judge is ready to summarise Humpty's case. In bullet points, list the points for and against the issue.

This is a **short** writing task, so you have 20 minutes to plan, write and check your writing.

HOW DID YOU DO?

1 This task was to write an argument in the form of a TV news report. The audience is the general public so your writing should be fairly formal. Even though it would be a spoken news report, you should still have organised your writing in paragraphs. You should also have followed the typical structure of an argument.

2 This task was to write an argument in the form of a bullet-pointed list. You still need to identify the issue but you could do that through the title or headings.

See page 63 for an example answer.

Check your writing against the text plan and key language features checklist on page 22.

WRITING FICTION

Achieved?

Fiction texts can be in the form of stories, plays or poems. Their purpose is to entertain a reader. In this section we are just concentrating on writing stories. All writers 'borrow' ideas from other writers. So... read! Note down ideas, sentences, phrases and words that you like. Use them in your writing.

There are three things that all stories have in common:

* Setting * Characters * Theme

- Page 25 of this book looks at the way stories are **structured**.

- Page 26 of this book looks at these story 'ingredients'. You need to put all three into the mixing pot to make a story.

- There is a section on each of the **ingredients** on pages 27–33. Each section gives you **hints, tips, ideas** and **examples**. There are also some practice questions. These are **short** writing tasks.

- But stories don't just happen. You need to plan ahead. Page 34 of this book looks at some planning ideas. **Planning** is important so don't skip this bit!

Over to you!

Work through each section carefully.
Make sure you understand what you need to tell the reader and how.
Have a go at the practice questions.
Look back at the section. Have you included the right sort of detail in the right sort of way?

Practice questions

On page 35 there are five fiction practice questions. These are **long** writing tasks. Remember – think, plan, write, check.

Hints

Keep a Writing Ideas Book. In this you can record all your ideas for writing fiction. These can be notes on character, setting and theme.

When you write, it's like having a film running in your head. Sometimes, it's easy to forget to tell the reader what is happening. So, your characters might move from the house to the park – tell the reader that the setting has changed. When your characters are talking to each other, tell the reader who is saying what. But above all – keep it simple!

WRITING FICTION 25

Story structure

All stories are organised in the same basic way. When you plan and write, think in five sections.

Beginning
Introduce the **main characters** and the **setting**.

Build up
The **story gets going** – the characters start to do something.

Problem
Something goes wrong for the characters. This is the most exciting part.

Resolution
The **problem is sorted** out in some way.

Ending
All the **loose ends are tied up.** The **characters reflect, or think,** about what happened.

Setting, Characters and Theme

Before even planning a story, you need to decide on the three main story ingredients.

Setting

This is WHEN and WHERE the story takes place. You need to help the reader to make a picture in their minds. The setting can also be used to create an atmosphere and affect how the reader feels.

Think about some stories you have read. When and where were they set? How do you know? Look at some short stories to see how the authors have told the reader about the setting. Have a go at drawing the setting that you read about.

There is more about story settings on pages 27 to 29.

Characters

This is WHO is in the story. You need to help the reader build up a picture of the main characters. They need to have an idea of what the characters are like.

Think about some stories you have read. Who were the characters? What were they like? How do you know? What were they called? Look at some short stories to see how authors have told the reader about the characters. Try drawing a character as you see them.

There is more about characters on pages 30 and 31.

Theme

This is WHAT happens in the story. Some people say that there are only a few story themes in the world. All writers borrow ideas from other stories and this is something you can do.

Think about some stories you have read. What happened? Did one story remind you of any others? List some of the common themes, e.g. good overcoming evil, main character losing something.

There is more about theme on pages 32 and 33.

Once you've chosen your ingredients, mix them together and make a story!

Setting

WRITING FICTION 27

Achieved?

Introduce the setting in the beginning section of the story. Remember the two key things that you need to tell your reader are when and where the story is set.

When?

The big picture
Is your story set in the past, now or in the future? Look at these three examples. How has the writer told the reader about the big picture?

- *The shiny, winged spaceships hovered above the glass towers of the city.*
- *The hooves of the horses pulling the coach clattered on the wet cobbles of the square.*  
- *Joe tucked his skateboard under his arm and walked out of the door.*

So, this writer used objects to tell us when the story was set. Spaceships and glass towers point to a story set in the future. Horse-drawn coaches and cobbles tell us this story is probably set in the past. The skateboard indicates that the story is set now.

The smaller picture
In what season or time of year is your story happening? Look how this writer tells us.

- *The warm summer sun peeped around the green curtains.*
- *Joe looked through the window and gasped. The ground was covered with a thin layer of snow.*
- *The buds on the trees were just starting to open.*
- *The children raced into the park, kicking their way through the piles of russet and gold and bronze leaves.*

This time the writer has used nature to tell us when the story was set. In the first example we are told that it is summer but in a more interesting way than saying 'It was a warm day in the summer.' The mention of snow makes winter the setting. Buds open in the spring and leaves fall in the autumn.

The even smaller picture

At what time of day is your story happening? Think about how you could tell your reader this information without being too obvious. Again, look at how this writer has done it.

- *The sun was just rising when Joe left the house.*
- *The sun was just setting when Joe returned.*
- *"Tea's ready," called Mum.*
- *The moon lay in the sky amid the scattered stars.*

Where?

Where is your story set? You need to give your reader an idea of what the place is like. This is where you can start to use the five senses:

- Sight
- Sound
- Touch
- Smell
- Taste (This is probably the hardest to use.)

Don't throw in all of the senses – it's too much for a reader to take in. Make it a rule to use **no more than three**. So, you might end up with something like this.

> **As Joe pushed open the huge wooden door he could see a large stone-floored hallway. He slipped through the doorway, cobwebs brushing his face. Once inside he breathed in the musty, damp smell of the old, empty house.**

Can you spot which three senses the writer has used?

If you are writing a short task that asks you to describe a setting, you can afford to put in a lot of detail. In a long task, where the setting is just one of the story ingredients, you need to introduce the setting in no more than three sentences. Don't worry about the big picture, the smaller picture and the even smaller picture. Go for where the story is set. Look at the example above again – that would be fine.

> ★ **Tip**
>
> Use a setting that you know. If your characters move from one setting to another, remember to tell your reader!

Text example

Setting description

> Pushing open the huge wooden door, Joe could see a large stone-floored hallway. He slipped through the doorway, cobwebs brushing his face. Once inside he breathed in the musty, damp smell of the old, empty house. He carefully placed his skateboard against the wall. The springtime morning sun shone weakly through the dusty windows and fell upon the shrouded furniture.

Practice questions

Write a setting description of one of the following places.

1. A fairytale castle
2. An empty football stadium
3. Your house
4. Your street
5. A deserted school

These are **short** writing tasks, so you have 20 minutes to plan, write and check your writing.

Characters

Achieved? 😊 😐 ☹

Introduce the main characters in the beginning section of the story. Have a clear idea of the characters in your own mind. You need to describe the characters':

- appearance
- voice
- movement

These three things should build up a picture of the character in the reader's mind.

Appearance

You can describe the characters face and hair, and their clothing and overall appearance. What do you think these characters are like? How has the writer made you feel that way?

- *Her wild ginger hair was held back with large green slides. She wore paint-spattered dungarees and, oddly, cycle clips around her ankles.*
- *His pale face and dark eyes stood out above the oil-stained dungarees. He glared at the group of young children.*

The writer has given us some description of the characters' appearance. Look at the use of adjectives. But, we also need to use what we already know about people to build up a picture of the characters.

Voice

Now we can add some dialogue. But the dialogue needs to move the story on – don't waste it on idle chit-chat! What has the writer done here?

Check this out:

- *Her wild ginger hair was held back with large green slides. She wore paint-spattered dungarees and, oddly, cycle clips around her ankles. "I've solved it," she announced proudly.*
- *His pale face and dark eyes stood out above the oil-stained dungarees. He glared at the group of young children. "Who?" he started. "Who has been fiddling with my bike?" he continued, his voice shaking with anger.*

Now how do you feel about the two characters? The writer has added dialogue and also used adverbs to tell us how the characters said it.

Make it very clear who is speaking. Use pronouns (he/she/they) and the characters' names. See pages 44 to 45 for further information about punctuating dialogue.

Movement

Now we're really motoring! We need to add some detail about how the characters move. How can the writer give us clues about the characters through movement?

- *Her wild ginger hair was held back with large green slides. She wore paint-spattered dungarees and, oddly, cycle clips around her ankles.*
  "I've solved it," she announced proudly. She strode confidently into the centre of the room.
- *His pale face and dark eyes stood out above the oil-stained dungarees. He glared at the group of young children.*
  "Who?" he started. "Who has been fiddling with my bike?" he continued, his voice shaking with anger. He stepped forwards, his fists clenched.

So, now how do you feel about the characters? Do you have an idea of what they are like? The writer has added some information about how they move. Look at the verbs the author has used to describe the movement.

Now read the descriptions and identify the words that tell you about the character.

Finally

You might want to think about your character's name. Names can often tell your reader a great deal about the character. Mrs Pinchnose sounds unpleasant, as does Curt Short. Why? On the other hand, Mrs Phunn and Mr Jolly sound quite nice! But why?

KEY FACT

If you are writing a short task that asks you to describe a character, you can afford to go into a lot of detail.

In a long task, where the characters are just one of the story ingredients, you need to introduce them quickly and then tell the reader what they are like through the three things we've been looking at. About two or three sentences should be enough.

★ Tip

Make the names suit the characters, for example Professor Scatty. Keep to two characters, three at most. If you have one male and one female, there is no confusion over pronouns (he/she). If you make one good and one bad, there is no confusion over who is who.

Theme

Achieved? 😊 😐 ☹

Here we are looking at just a few story themes. You could try writing each of them or really concentrating on perhaps two. Make sure that you have the structure of each theme really clear in your head.

Good overcomes evil

What stories can you think of where this is the theme? Snow White and Jack the Giant Killer are examples. So are the Harry Potter stories. But you don't have time in the National Tests to write a Harry Potter! The basic structure goes something like this:

Beginning	Two main characters are introduced – one good and one evil. Setting is established.
Build up	Good character is innocently going about normal life. Evil character is plotting and scheming.
Problem	Evil character tricks and threatens to harm good character.
Resolution	Good character outwits evil character.
Ending	Everything is OK. The characters reflect or think about what happened.

Once you've got the hang of the structure you can start to experiment. You might write a story about a person overcoming a fear or a bully. It's still a similar structure.

Lost or found

Again, think of stories that you know where the main character either loses or finds something or somebody, e.g. The Lord of the Rings. This type of story might look like this:

Beginning	Introduce one main character and establish the setting.
Build up	The story gets going – the character starts to do something quite normal.
Problem	The character finds or loses something or someone (could be the second main character).
Resolution	The lost thing/person is returned. The found thing/person turns out to be not quite what it seemed.
Ending	Everything is OK. The characters reflect or think about what happened.

How could you use this structure and theme in a slightly different way? A story about someone dying or losing their sight is pretty serious stuff but it's still the same basic structure.

Wishing or wanting

Traditional tales often have these themes, e.g. Cinderella. But you could write modern versions.

Beginning	Introduce the main character and establish the setting. Identify what the main character is wishing for or wanting.
Build up	The character goes in search of their wish.
Problem	The character is stopped from getting what they want, perhaps by a second character.
Resolution	The character gets what they want.
Ending	The character reflects on whether getting their wish was really worth it.

WRITING FICTION

Planning

Achieved? 😊 😐 ☹

Planning is a very useful way of thinking about the story ingredients and organising ideas. In the long SATs writing task you only have about 10 minutes planning time – not very long at all!

So, you need to develop a way of planning that is fast and works for you. Try using the five box plan below. Make sure you know the heading for each box and the main things that need to be in that section of the story.

Five box plan

Heading	Main things to include	Example
Beginning	Introduce main character Setting	Joe, boy about 11, into skateboarding. Old empty house, bit spooky.
Build up	Story gets going	Joe goes into house. Looking for something. Sees pawprints.
Problem	Something goes wrong	Can hear cat but can't get to it. Cat stuck behind wall.
Resolution	Problems sorted out	Joe finds secret button to open wall. Rescues cat.
Ending	Loose ends tied up Characters reflect or think	Everything OK. Joe and cat go off on skateboard.

Now it's just a case of turning your plan into a story. But please remember to refer to your plan while you are writing – don't write something completely different!

1. Practise quickly drawing out the five box plan and adding the headings. This should take no more than 30 seconds!

2. Now look back at the main things to include. Practise adding the main things to your five boxes. This should take another 30 seconds.

3. Next practise planning actual stories (you don't need to write them at this stage). Look at some of the long tasks on page 35. Read the task carefully, then re-read it. Got an idea? Go!

4. Think about the story ingredients you could include. Remember – **characters, setting, theme**. Spend no more than four minutes on this. You've now used five minutes of your planning time.

5. Make notes about the ingredients in the boxes. Remember, these are notes – not sentences! You are not writing the story here – you are planning it. Five minutes later – time's up!

Putting it all together

So, you know the three story ingredients (characters, theme, setting), you know the structure and you know how to plan (five box plan). It's just a case of putting it all together in a short story.

Remember, in a long writing task you have 10 minutes' planning time and 35 minutes' writing time. This is not very long. You can't afford to have too much detail or make the characters have great adventures. Keep it simple!

Look at this example. It's about the right length and includes all the story ingredients that you've been reading about.

The empty house

As Joe pushed open the huge wooden door he could see a large stone-floored hallway. He slipped through the doorway, cobwebs brushing his face. Once inside he breathed in the musty, damp smell of the old, empty house.

"Hello!" he called. "Is anyone there?" All he heard was his own voice echoing around the hall. Looking at the floor he could see paw prints in the dust. He moved forward, tracking them like a hunter in a desert. Then, suddenly, they stopped. Joe found himself staring at a blank wall. There were no more paw prints to be seen.

"Cinders can't have disappeared into thin air," he said to himself. "Cats don't do that."

He paused and held his breath. He thought he could hear a faint meowing. He listened hard. His black eyes stood out in his pale face as he knelt down on the floor and put his ear to the wall. Finally his face brightened as he started tapping at the wall.

With a creak a panel in the wall started to move. The meowing grew louder and Joe's smile grew wider. Eventually the gap in the wall was big enough to reveal... Cinders, Joe's little black cat.

"Oh Cinders, how did you get in there?" asked Joe. Cinders arched her back and purred.

"Come on, let's go," Joe said. He picked up his skateboard as the pair left the empty house. Placing it on the ground, he patted the front. Cinders jumped on and sat up straight, looking like the proudest cat in town. Joe hopped on behind her and they sped off down the street.

"That's the last time I let you go mouse hunting in there!" Joe told his cat. Cinders blinked and didn't make a sound.

Practice questions

These are **long** writing tasks, so you have 10 minutes to think and plan and 35 minutes to write and check your writing.

1. This is the opening sentence of a story. Write a story that could follow it.

    The shiny, winged space ships hovered above the glass towers of the city.

2. Write a story for younger children about a character who finds something unusual in a park.

3. This is the closing sentence of a story. Write a story that could end with it.

    The hooves of the horses pulling the coach clattered on the wet cobbles of the square.

4. Write a story with these ingredients: an old woman, a young boy, a castle, good overcomes evil.

5. This is the opening sentence of a story. Write a story that could follow it.

    Joe tucked his skateboard under his arm and walked out of the door.

GRAMMAR

INTRODUCTION

So you've got the hang of writing non-fiction and stories. You know how to organise your writing, what to include and what not to include. Polishing up your grammar could make that final difference to your writing.

In a Level 4 piece of writing, the writer needs to:

- use different types of SENTENCES and PUNCTUATE them correctly;
- organise writing into PARAGRAPHS;
- use a variety of suitable CONNECTIVES;
- choose VOCABULARY carefully.

When you are reading, look carefully at how writers use grammar. Remember, you can 'borrow' their ideas and use them in your writing.

SENTENCES

Remember, you need to use different types of SENTENCES and PUNCTUATE them correctly.

KEY FACTS

- Sentences start with a capital letter and end with a full stop (.), question mark (?) or exclamation mark (!).
- A sentence is made up of one or more clauses.
- There are three main types of sentence – simple, compound and complex. You can use them in different ways to have an effect on your reader.

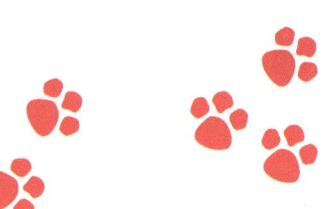

Three types of sentences

Simple sentences

As the name suggests, simple sentences are easy to write and read.
They have one clause: *It was raining.*

⭐ Using lots of simple sentences can be very boring for a reader.
I went out. It was raining hard. I put up my brolly. I saw my friend Daisy. I called loudly to her. She came over.

⭐ These sentences aren't interesting for a reader because they are all the same length.
Can you think of and write down your own simple sentence?

```
[                                                              ]
```

Compound sentences

Compound sentences have two or more clauses that are as important as each other. They can be joined by these connectives:

and   like   but   so

It was raining hard so I put up my brolly.

Now make your simple sentence into a compound sentence.

```
[                                                              ]
```

Be careful that you don't always use *and* to join two clauses.
Learn the connectives in the list so that you can use all of them.

Complex sentences

Complex sentences have two or more clauses that are as important as each other and another clause that is less important! This is called a subordinate clause and is linked to the main sentence with a subordinating connective. For example:

after	if	unless
although	in case	until
as	once	when
because	since	while
before	though	

When I left the house, I found that it was raining hard so I put up my brolly.

```
[                                                              ]
```

Try making your compound sentence into a complex sentence.
Learn some of the connectives in the list and try to use them in your writing.

Mixing sentences

Sentence types
Any writing becomes boring if you use the same type of sentence all the time. You need to use a mix.

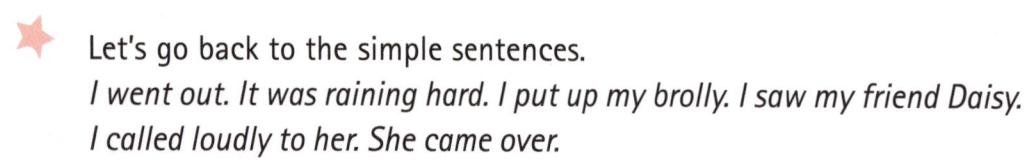

- Let's go back to the simple sentences.
  I went out. It was raining hard. I put up my brolly. I saw my friend Daisy. I called loudly to her. She came over.

- How can they be improved?
  I went out. It was raining hard so I put up my brolly. As I was struggling with the catch, I saw my friend Daisy. I called loudly to her. She came over, splashing through the puddles on her way.

Well, it does sound better doesn't it? Can you spot what's changed? Changing the sentence types means that the reader is given more detail too.

Using questions
You can have your characters asking questions when they are speaking but try asking questions in other parts of the story too.

- *Joe could just see something through the mist, but what was it?*
- *Why was the table shaking?*
- *How would Jake get out of this fix?*

Asking questions means that the reader becomes more interested in the story.

Using exclamations
Again, you can have your characters exclaiming when they speak. You can also use exclamations to make part of a story more exciting.

- *It spoke!*
- *She was stuck!*
- *He jumped!*

How do they do it?

Let's look at how two children's authors use different sentence types.

The Locket

He didn't look back. He set sail into the night, delighted with his daring exploits and laughing with excitement at the thought of the riches he knew would be his. Halfway into his voyage home, he could contain himself no longer and he opened the locket.

- The author has used all three sentence types in this extract.

Secrets and eyes

My thirst satisfied, I looked down at the boy in faded Bermuda shorts who had taken my money. He looked at me cautiously with eyes that held the secrets of someone twice his age.

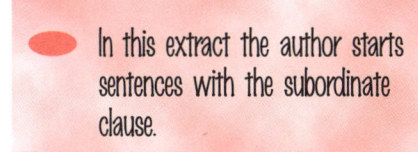

- In this extract the author starts sentences with the subordinate clause.

Practice questions

Take the first extract and write a paragraph about the character.

- Write about where the character had been and what he had done.
- Describe the contents of the locket and his reaction to it in a compound sentence.
- Use a simple sentence to keep the reader in suspense.

★ Look at books in your classroom. Can you find examples of authors who have used different sentence types in their writing?

★ Try using some of their sentences as models for your own writing.

PARAGRAPHS

Remember, you need to organise your writing into paragraphs.

Paragraphs help writers to organise their thoughts, and help readers to follow the story-line, argument or dialogue.

In non-fiction, starting a new paragraph shows the reader that:
- a new area of the subject is being introduced
- time has moved forward or back e.g. *By the end of 1999...*

In stories you start a new paragraph when:
- there is a change in time
- the setting has changed
- a change of speaker in a passage of dialogue
- there is a new event or change of scene
- a new character appears

Example

Kelly could still make out the words in the darkness, "Children must be accompanied by an adult" in letters that swirled across the glossy painted board.

"How appropriate!" mocked a man's voice from somewhere very close. Kelly turned her head slowly towards the sound.

"Is that you Dad?" As soon as the words left her mouth, she spun on her heels.

Without waiting for a reply, Kelly ran blindly into the darkness, her feet barely touching the worn, flattened grass, as the feeling of panic took over.

Ten minutes later she was still running. Her heart was pounding and the voice was getting closer.

New paragraph:
Something new is happening.

New paragraph:
There is a new speaker.

New paragraph:
Something new is happening.

New paragraph:
Time has moved forward.

Practice questions

Look at some of the long writing tasks in the non-fiction section and the fiction section.

Plan the paragraphs that you would include.

Look back at the writing that you did for the practice questions. Do your paragraphs work?

★ Tips
- Read two pages of your reading book. At the end of each paragraph, make a note of the main focus.
- How is the writer moving the narrative on?

CONNECTIVES

Remember, when you write should use a variety of suitable CONNECTIVES.

Connectives are words that link clauses or sentences.

There are different connectives for different purposes. If you look back at the non-fiction section on pages 10 to 23, the types of connective that you can use for each text type are listed. When you are writing stories, you usually use time connectives. When you are writing you need to make sure that you use a variety of suitable connectives. Using AND THEN time after time is very boring for a reader.

Addition

We often write AND or AND THEN.

You could try these:
- also
- furthermore
- moreover

Against

We often write BUT.

You could try:
- however
- on the other hand
- nevertheless

Time

We often write THEN or AND THEN.

You could try these:
- first
- next
- just then
- meanwhile
- when
- once
- after that
- later
- finally

★ Tips

- Look at some books.
- Find the connectives.
- Start connectives lists.
- Learn some of the words.
- Make sure that you use a variety of suitable connectives when you write.

Cause and effect

We often write BECAUSE.

You could try these:
- as
- so
- so that
- in order to
- this means that
- consequently
- as a result

Logical

We often write BECAUSE or SO.

You could try these:
- therefore
- furthermore
- consequently
- thus

Summing up

We often write FINALLY.

You could try these:
- in conclusion
- to summarise
- as a result

Practice questions

Use these connectives to create compound sentences from the following simple sentences:

because, although, despite the fact, until

a) The day began well. It started to pour down with torrential rain.

b) The blossom makes the garden look beautiful. It only lasts for a couple of weeks.

c) My sister's room is a mess. She never takes the time to tidy it up.

d) The ravenous lion continued to eat. It had been eating for over an hour.

HOW DID YOU DO?

See page 63 for an example answer.

PUNCTUATION

Punctuation is the voice of your writing. When you write you need to PUNCTUATE your sentences correctly. This means using full stops, question marks, exclamation marks, commas, apostrophes and speech punctuation in the right places.

Punctuation allows you to mark your writing so that the reader knows how to read it.

Read these words out loud. How does the punctuation change the meaning?

- Now.
- Now!
- Now?
- Now...

Sentences – the basics

- Every sentence should start with a capital letter and end with a full stop (.), question mark (?) or exclamation mark (!).
- Names of people, places, days of the week and months of the year all start with a capital letter. Make sure that your capitals are clear and look different from your lower case letters. Write out the alphabet in capitals, then in lower case, to check that they are clearly different.

Practice questions

Rewrite these with the correct punctuation.

a) sam thought that london was a very noisy city

b) where was that cat

c) it was a windy monday in march when kylie first met jack

See page 63 for an example answer.

HOW DID YOU DO?

COMMAS

A comma is a punctuation mark that separates a part of a sentence. Commas are used:

- to separate names, adjectives or items in a list –
  They took crisps, sandwiches and a bottle of lemonade to the park.
  OR
  Bobby, George, Dennis and Alex were all members of the winning team.
  Notice that you don't need a comma before the last item in the list. Use 'and' instead.
- to give extra information – *Mr Cooper, my teacher, is leaving next week.*
- after a subordinate clause – *In spite of the number of guards, he still managed to escape.*

Try saying a sentence out loud before you write it down. It will help you to 'hear' where the commas should go.

Practice questions

1) The dog's feet had been dried but it still managed to tread soil onto the carpet.
2) Even though they were excited the children were very well behaved at the carnival.
3) Looking down into the bath water she could see that the glitter had risen to the surface and was stuck to her legs.
4) Until she was old enough my younger sister was not allowed to go out by herself.

HOW DID YOU DO?

See page 63 for an example answer.

SPEECH PUNCTUATION

There are two ways of telling a reader what a character says.

Indirect speech

You can report what was said without using the exact words of the speaker. You don't need to use speech marks:

Flora said that she was going out.
Mum whispered to me that she was very excited.
Jack threatened that he would scream if they didn't leave him alone.

Direct speech

You can use the speaker's actual words inside speech marks (" "). But, there's a bit more punctuation needed – usually a comma.

Look at these examples and think about where the comma is put.
"I'm going out," said Flora.
"I'm very excited," whispered Mum.

Here, the comma is used at the end of the speech INSIDE the last speech mark, before the speaker and the speech verb.

If you start the sentence with the speaker and the speech verb, the comma comes before the first speech mark. Also, the speech starts with a capital letter.

Flora said, "I'm going out."
Mum whispered, "I'm very excited."
Jack threatened, "Leave me alone or I'll scream."

If the speaker and speech verb are in the middle of the speech, then the second section of speech does not start with a capital letter because it's all one sentence.

"Leave me alone," Jack yelled, "or I'll scream."

Look at the position of the commas in the example too.

Full stops, commas, question marks and exclamation marks must be placed within the speech marks.

"Go away!" she screamed.
"Are you all right?" he asked.

And finally – new speaker = new line.
To make it easier for the reader to see who is speaking, start a new line when a new speaker speaks.

"And where," Dad asked, "do you think you've been?"
"At the park," Lauren answered, looking him in the eye.
"The park?"
"Yes!" she replied.

APOSTROPHES

Apostrophes can cause catastrophes! When used incorrectly they can change the meaning of a sentence. There are two reasons why you use apostrophes:
- to show that something belongs to somebody (possession)
- to show that a letter has been missed out (omission)

Possession

Kelly's car – meaning the car belonging to Kelly.
Mum's shoes – meaning the shoes belonging to Mum.

Be careful if the noun is in the plural – more than one.
   The boys' jackets. (plural)
   The boy's jacket. (singular)
Can you spot the difference?

Omission

Could not becomes *couldn't*
Does not becomes *doesn't*.

It might help you to read the two words out loud. If you are missing out a letter, you need an apostrophe.

Practice questions

1 The following are shortened forms (contractions) of two words. Write them out in full:

I'm	I am
isn't	
couldn't	
don't	
he's	
they've	
we'll	

2 Write out the contracted form of these words.

has not	hasn't
did not	
you are	
I would	
we have	
it is	
we are	

PUNCTUATION

Practice questions

Add the apostrophe to these examples.

1) The mans bicycle stood against the wall.
2) The cows horn had to be cut short.
3) The girls shoes were too tight. (one girl)
4) The boys pencils were the same. (two boys)
5) The dogs tail wagged happily at his owner.
6) The dragons talons scratched at each other's faces. (two dragons)
7) The childs book was torn in two.
8) Volcanoes lava can travel at terrific speeds. (two volcanoes)
9) A rivers journey comes to its end at the sea.
10) Trees branches swayed and rustled as the storm approached. (more than one tree)

Look through books that you are reading to find examples of apostrophes and work out whether they are of possession or omission.

Practice questions

Now it's time to put all this punctuation into practice.

All of the punctuation has been taken out of this passage. Your challenge is to put it back in. Read it through carefully before you start. It will make you realise how hard it is to read without any punctuation!

suddenly a strange gnarled little man appeared from nowhere he had a long white beard filled with seaweed and boots made from sea shells who are you gasped the fisherman his eyes widening the tiny man jumped up onto the boat you must be handsomely rewarded he said to the fisherman

There are: 5 full stops   2 sets of speech marks
            5 capital letters   1 question mark
            4 commas

HOW DID YOU DO? See page 63 for an example answer.

VOCABULARY

Achieved?

Think about the words you are going to use in your writing. If you choose them well they can improve the standard of your writing. They can give your reader a clear picture of what you mean, and you will get your message across.

Remember – try to avoid repeating favourite words in a single piece of writing.

ADJECTIVES

Adjectives are used to describe a noun. They describe something or someone.
A red door.
A crying child.

Hints and tips

- Avoid using adjectives that say the same thing.
  A frozen, icy lake.

- Instead, use two adjectives that say something different.
  A vast icy lake.

- Avoid adjectives in your writing that you use when chatting, for example *really, very, nice, OK*.
  We all ate a really nice meal is dull.
  We all ate a delicious meal is better.

- Adjectives that have the same initial sound as the noun work well in poetry and fiction. This is called **alliteration**.
  The magical music.

- Remember – only use factual adjectives in non-fiction. Use them to add information.
  The white football rather than *the gloriously gleaming white football*.

Practice questions

Change these adjectives to give readers a better picture.

- This is a GOOD story. _____
- The train had NICE PURPLE doors. _____
- After the race his face was VERY RED. _____
- Mrs Smith is REALLY CROSS. _____
- The tree had BIG flowers on its branches. _____

ADVERBS

Adverbs are used to describe a verb. They describe how something is said or done.
He gripped tightly.
"I think so," he answered quietly.

Look again at the section on characters on pages 30 to 31 to find more about using adverbs in speech.

Practice questions

Choose an adverb to make these sentences more interesting.

- He banged the book onto the table. _____
- "You look out!" he whispered. _____
- The monkey climbed from branch to branch. _____
- "It wasn't me!" she said. _____

VERBS

Verbs tell us what someone or something is doing. Choose your verbs well and it can improve your writing. Which sentence do you think gives a better picture of what is happening?

Daisy put the shoe back into the box.
Daisy slammed the shoe back into the box.

Martin got his hat and raced to the door.
Martin grabbed his hat and raced to the door.

Avoid using *put* or *get* if you can. They don't tell the reader very much about what is happening.

Practice questions

Choose a new verb to add interest to these sentences.

1) Hoards of menacing monkeys *swung* through the high treetops. _____
2) The proud princess *walked* along the streets of cheering crowds. _____
3) She *put* the china cups carefully in the basket. _____
4) The thief *got* through the broken attic window. _____

> ★ **Tip**
>
> In the National Tests you need to show that you can make good vocabulary choices. Have a go at different words. If you get the spelling wrong, you'll still get more marks for good vocabulary than you lose for a wrong spelling.

SPELLING

Achieved?

The Spelling Test lasts for ten minutes. You will be asked to spell 20 words from a passage that your teacher reads to you.

The test will cover:
- basic spelling rules;
- more difficult or unusual words that might not fit the basic spelling rules.

KEY FACTS

This is a list of the 20 most frequently misspelt words in the National Tests over the last few years. Make sure you get them right this year!

change	nastiest	technique	stripes
advertise	designed	swimming	perfectly
injured	regardless	ready	future
serious	attempts	vanishing	produce
surprise	individual	known	themselves

The spelling rules that follow will help you. Read through and make sure you understand them. Then remember to use them when you write.

PLURALS

- Most words – just add *s*. *Road – roads, cup – cups, book – books, cat – cats.*
- Some words need *es* to be added. Say them aloud and listen to how they sound. Words that end in a hissing or buzzing sound follow this rule. *Box – boxes, bus – buses, watch – watches.* Words ending in *x, z, ch, sh,* and *s* usually follow this pattern.
- Words that end in *f* have a different pattern. You usually need to drop the *f* and add *ves*. *Hoof – hooves, wolf – wolves.* But beware! There are exceptions. *Gulf – gulfs, roof – roofs, dwarf – dwarfs.* Try to learn these words.
- Words that end in *y* have a simple rule.
  - If the letter before *y* is a vowel (*a e i o u*), just add *s*. *Way – ways, toy – toys, monkey – monkeys.*
  - If any other letters come before the *y* (consonants), drop the *y* and add *ies*. *Lady – ladies, spy – spies, story – stories.*
- Learn the irregular words. *Mouse – mice, man – men, child – children.* When you are reading, make a note of any irregular plurals you find and learn them.

Practice questions

Change these words into plurals.

1. fox, road, bunch, wish, sound, life, tax, tree, drink, pirate, house, donkey, fly, bus

2. Look through books or dictionaries and find words ending in y, x, z, s. Change them into plurals.

HOW DID YOU DO? See page 63 for an example answer.

DOUBLING THE CONSONANT

There is a simple rule to help you spell words that end in a consonant when you add *er*, *ed* or *ing*. Listen to the sound the vowel makes.

Vowels can make short sounds or long sounds.
- *Stop* has a short 'o' sound.
- *Boat* has a long 'o' sound.

The rule is: double the consonant if the sound is short.
Stop - stopping, boat - boating.

Practice questions

- Write these words in two lists. Put all the words with short vowel sounds in one list, and all the long vowel sounds in the other list.

    bin, line, paper, chat, choose, flutter, reign, wet, meet, light, float, dot

- Look through some books and add four new words to each list.
- Add an ending *ing*, *er* or *ed* to the words to make a different word.
- Check the vowel sound to see which words need to have a double consonant.
- Check your spelling in a dictionary.

HOW DID YOU DO?
See page 63 for an example answer.

LONG VOWELS

Words with long vowel sounds can be spelt in different ways.
Make sure you know the spelling patterns.

A   *Rake, rain, play. ai* usually comes in the middle of words.

E   *Peel, team, thief, here.*

I   *Fine, sky, light.*

O   *Bone, coat, slow. oa* usually comes in the middle of words.

U   *Cube. u-e* words have a slightly different sound. You also need to learn the spelling pattern of long *oo* words, like *blue*, *blew* and *hoot*.

> Draw some columns on a sheet of paper, or use a computer. Write a long vowel spelling pattern at the top of each column. Look through some books and add words to each column to match the spelling pattern. Watch out for exceptions and learn them.

SPELLING RULES

Tenses

Put these verbs into the past, present and future tenses. It is a good way to practise many of the spelling rules. If you find spelling some of them hard, look back at the spelling rules and learn them. If you still have trouble getting them right, read as much as you can and practise all you can. Check your answers on page 64.

Verb	Past tense	Present tense	Future tense
To fit	I have fitted, I fitted, I was fitting	I fit, I am fitting	I will fit
To move			
To bite			
To clap			
To keep			
To swim			
To light			
To fly			
To injure			
To watch			
To produce			
To dance			
To try			
To pursue			
To cheat			

THE SPELLING TEST!

After learning all the facts and spelling rules on the previous pages, have a go at these questions. If you double your final score you will have your percentage. A good estimate for a Level 4 will be over 70%. Check your answers on page 64.

Section A

Spell the plural of these words:

1. crunch _____
2. aunt _____
3. tax _____
4. hippy _____
5. werewolf _____
6. lunch _____
7. pony _____
8. chair _____
9. sofa _____
10. hippopotamus _____

Section B

Correctly add 'ing' to these words:

1. bat _____
2. trot _____
3. shoot _____
4. weep _____
5. sleep _____

Correctly add 'ed' to these words:

1. snort _____
2. look _____
3. map _____
4. slap _____
5. shop _____

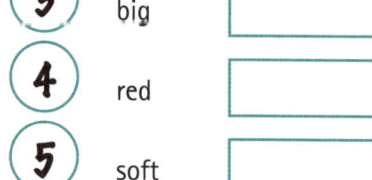

Correctly add 'er' to these words:

1. strong _____
2. loud _____
3. big _____
4. red _____
5. soft _____

Section C

Read the clues then correctly spell the answers:

1. The past tense of 'I brake' _____
2. The future tense of 'I grew' _____
3. The past tense of 'I will sharpen' _____
4. The present tense of 'I will skip' _____
5. Zebras and tigers have them – 's_____'
6. A female actor is called an 'a_____'
7. It is a well k_____ fact!
8. The slipper fitted p_____.
9. Ali Baba and the 40 t_____.
10. Elizabeth I r_____ for 45 years.

Section D

The words in italics have been spelt incorrectly. Write down the correct spelling.

Dinosaws have been *extinged* for over 60 million years. Nobody knows *eggsactly* why they died out so suddenly. Some *siontists* think a *jyant* asteroid hit the Earth and filled the *atmosfear* with dense clouds of dust. These clouds blocked the sun's rays and the cold-blooded *creeches* could not adapt to the new *condishuns*. However, smaller animals such as mammals and *insex* were more *adapptuble* and became the new rulers of the Earth. There are still many species which have *sirvyved* from the time before the mass extinction. Crocodiles and sharks are very *sucksessfull* predators and have *xissded* on Earth for over 200 million years. Humans have only been around for about 2 million years. We are *probubbly* more of a threat to the *curant* species on the planet than any impact from outer space.

REVIEWING YOUR WORK

Re-reading, or reviewing, your work is an important part of being a writer. No writer thinks their work is finished without re-reading it and checking it makes sense. Don't worry if you find things that need changing – there are always changes to be made. It is a good opportunity to look at ways in which your writing could be improved.

Here are some ideas to keep in mind when you are reviewing your work.

* **Make sure your reader will understand your main message.** For example, if you are writing a mystery story, will your reader want to find out what happens? Ask yourself if you have given too many clues to the ending. Is there a feeling of suspense and excitement? If you are writing an explanation, have you used connectives to help the reader follow the process that you are explaining? Would you be able to understand the explanation easily? If you are not sure, have another look at the guidelines for writing explanations.

* **Make sure you have followed the guidelines for the text type you are writing.** If you are not sure, go back and check. Keep the style constant, and try not to slip from one type of writing to another. If you started in the first person voice, have you kept to it all the way through your writing? Have you kept the same verb tense throughout? Don't get worried if you find mistakes, just correct them and try to remember for the future. No one gets it right all the time, but reviewing your work helps you to spot the errors that could lose you marks.

* **Check your spelling and grammar.** Look carefully as you read and, if a word doesn't look right, try it out on a piece of paper a few times. If you can, look it up in a dictionary, and try to learn the correct spelling for the future. Read your sentences aloud if you can. This will help you to hear when something doesn't sound right. If you think your grammar is not quite right, try saying the sentence in different ways, and re-write it a few times. Pick the one you think sounds best, and don't be afraid to make changes.

* **Read as often as you can.** Reading helps you become familiar with good writing, helps you recognise spelling patterns and helps you learn how to structure your sentences. Read as many kinds of books as you can. This will help you to get ideas to use in your own writing.

* **Keep a notebook and write down ideas, phrases, sentences and words that you like.** If you read a phrase that might be useful, don't be afraid to make use of it. You can learn a lot from other writers' ideas. Jot them down in your writer's notebook. You never know when they might come in handy.

READING COMPREHENSION

Achieved?

Reading the text

When you read a piece of text, don't rush. Try to enjoy it and immerse yourself in the story or information that is being given to you. When you have finished, take a minute to think and reflect on what you have read. Does it make sense? Did you understand what the author was saying? Authors often give clues in their writing and you have to find them. Good writers can leave things out and still get their message across.

Look at the following example:

> Josh cried long and deep into his hands. The lead hung from his pocket like a wilted flower and the chewed tennis ball was still wet from its last game with Spike. Had this actually happened? The smell of burnt tyres and the angry face of the driver told him it had.

1. What was hanging from Josh's pocket? *The answer to this can be searched for and found in the text – the lead!*

2. What or who is Spike? *The text doesn't actually say Spike is a dog but from reading the clues (lead and chewed tennis ball) it becomes quite clear.*

3. What do think has just happened? *Again, the text doesn't actually say but you can read the clues and come to a conclusion. Spike has been hit by a vehicle which had to brake suddenly, maybe to avoid him. He must be badly hurt because Josh is very upset and can't believe what's happened.*

Reading between the lines

'Deduction' and 'inference' are two words you need to understand when tackling reading comprehension texts.

- To 'deduce' means you use evidence in the text to understand what the author is telling you. For example, the 'smell of burnt tyres' is evidence that the driver has made an emergency stop.

- To 'infer' means that you use your own knowledge and the evidence in the text to come to a conclusion which goes beyond the information given. For example, 'the angry face of the driver' so we can infer that Spike caused the accident by running into the road.

ABOUT THE READING TEST

In the test, you should read the questions very carefully so that you fully understand what you are being asked.

You will be expected to:

- make sense of what you are reading
- find information and ideas in a text
- work out what the author meant
- work out why a text is organised in a particular way
- say something about the vocabulary and style that an author has used
- say something about how a text makes you feel
- link what you read to your own life.

★ Tips

- In your reading test, the questions ask for 1-, 2- or 3-mark answers.
- If an answer is worth 1 mark, you can often find the answer written on the page. You are being asked to find a particular word, phrase or piece of information. These questions are obviously the easiest but you still need to read and answer them carefully.
- If an answer is worth 2 or 3 marks, you are being asked to work out what the author meant. These questions are obviously harder but you get more marks!
- Always support your 2- and 3-mark answers with evidence and examples from the text.
- If you get a question that starts "What do you think..." or "How do you know...", you are being asked for your opinion. Always use examples from the text to back up your answer.

'Here be dragons!' ...

The Komodo dragons are alive and well in Indonesia – not the fire-breathing, winged wonders from myths and legends, but their close cousins. Here is some information about them.

Facts

Kingdom	Animalia
Phylum	Chordata
Class	Reptilia
Order	Squamata
Family	Varanidae
Genus	*Varanus*
Size	Female length: less than 2 m
	Male length: up to 3 m
Weight	Males: up to 135 kg
	Females: less than 50 kg

Description

The Komodo dragons are the largest lizards in the world and, with their ancient appearance and evocative name, they conjure up the stuff of legends. The heavy-set body is long with stocky legs and a long muscular tail; the scaly skin is greyish-brown all over. Dragons from the island of Flores, however, are earthen-red in colour with a yellow head. Juveniles have a more striking pattern with highly variable combinations of bands and speckling in yellow, green, grey and brown. Their long, forked yellow tongues resemble those of the mythical, fire-breathing dragons which gave them their name.

Range

Numerous on the island of Komodo in Indonesia, from which they have received their common name, these dragons are also found on the neighbouring islands of Rinca and Flores in Indonesia.

Habitat

The three islands where Komodo dragons live are all volcanic. They inhabit the lower monsoon forests and savannah up to about 700 metres above sea level.

Diet

Adult Komodo dragons are generally solitary, although groups may gather around a kill. They are powerful predators and their voracious appetite has further enhanced their ferocious image. Both carrion and live prey are consumed; adults ambush deer, water buffalo and wild pigs, and carcasses can be detected from up to 10 km away. Their large powerful jaws tear at prey and large amounts can be eaten with surprising speed. Only a small percentage of the kill is discarded. Komodo dragons can eat up to 80% of their own body weight at one time. The dragon's saliva can contain up to 50 different types of bacteria, probably as a result of eating carrion. The bite is therefore highly infectious, and even if the attacked prey escapes it is likely to die of blood poisoning within the week.

Life cycle
Komodo dragons mate during the dry season, which occurs between May and August. The males compete for the attention of the females by engaging in fierce battles. They wrestle upright, using their tails for support, grabbing each other with their front limbs and attempting to throw their opponent to the ground. The loser is the first dragon to fall.

Threats
The population of Komodo dragons today is estimated to be a mere fraction of its size 50 years ago. Causes of this decline are widespread habitat loss throughout the region, a loss of prey species and hunting. No Komodo dragons have been seen on the island of Padar since the 1970s, the result of widespread poaching of the deer that constitute their chief prey source.

Conservation
Komodo and surrounding islands lie within the Komodo National Park. Law has protected these dragons since the 1930s, and international trade is prohibited by their listing on Appendix I of the Convention on International Trade in Endangered Species (CITES). An important tourist trade has developed because of these spectacular creatures, bringing over 18,000 visitors to the area each year; it is hoped that this economic incentive will help to safeguard the future of these awesome dragons.

Practice questions

1) Up to what length can a male Komodo dragon grow? *(1 mark)*

2) How does the skin colour of the dragons from the island of Flores differ from that of the dragons from Komodo? *(1 mark)*

3) On which three islands do the dragons live? *(1 mark)*

4) On what do the adult dragons feed? *(1 mark)*

5) Explain why prey which has been attacked by a Komodo dragon is likely to die even if it escapes. *(2 marks)*

6) Why does the author use the word 'wrestle' to describe the way in which male dragons compete for the attention of females? *(2 marks)*

7) Describe three actions that you think could be taken to halt the decline in populations of the Komodo dragon. *(3 marks)*

8) Why do you think these creatures have been named 'dragons'? *(3 marks)*

How did you do?
See page 64 for an example answer.

Smile

Geraldine McCaughrean

Chapter 1

Suddenly he was falling, and his life went past in small, square pictures, framed in the windows of the cockpit. There were his family; his house, his friends, his wedding, his dog. There were pictures of the Past and pictures of the Future, too – all the things he had meant to do and now never would; bridges, faces, dawns and sunsets.

There were flames, as well, but they were not imaginary. They were running their orange tongues over the glass, licking away the views, gobbling up the sky. Flash would have liked to bid someone goodbye, but he was all alone in the plane.

The next he knew the windows were full of desert; red gulches and yellow valleys and salt-white lakes. The landscapes were so beautiful and so strange that Flash wanted to capture them, trap them like rare, free-flying birds. He wanted to photograph them.

No time for developer and fixer. No time for darkrooms and prints. His hands closed around the only camera of any use to him.

Then the plane tilted and it was too late. The scenes framed in its windows flickered by too fast to focus upon. As a cinema film rattles free of its spool, so Flash's fall rattled to an end. The crashing aeroplane landed in a sea of grey-green trees, folding its wings upwards like a butterfly. Branches broke through the floor. Leaves burst into the cockpit. The glass windows crazed like eggshell. If Flash had not been thrown out through the shattering roof, his life would have finished then and there. The End.

He fell heels-over-heart into a clump of thorn bushes. Just once his eyelids blinked, like a camera shutter, and took in the sight of his aeroplane burning, raised aloft on the arms of three blazing trees. In his head, he titled the picture 'Scorching the Sky'. Then his eyes closed and he returned to a darkroom empty of pictures, or even of dreams.

Chapter 2

"Who are you?" he asked.

"That's not hard. I know that," said the little girl. "What I don't know is who you are."

She was poking long, straight branches up the legs of his trousers, and Flash felt mildly annoyed to be woken only in time to be spit-roasted.

"Olu and I, we take you home," said the girl. She had dusky, dusty skin the colour of milky tea, and a scarlet dress. Her long, ragged hair was dusty too. It brushed Flash's face as she pushed the branches on through his shirt and out at the collar. Then she waved to the little boy to take his place by Flash's head.

When Flash realised what they were doing, he marvelled at their cleverness. Wonderful! That these primitive people should know, so young, how to transport an injured man across hostile wilderness. They balanced something on his stomach, then they both took hold of the ends of the two branches and lifted Flash clear of the ground.

All the buttons burst from his shirt and his head hit the ground with a thud. The camera on his stomach rolled down and smacked him in the face.

"I say to Olu, I say it won't work," said the girl, sagging under the weight of his body and legs. Any moment now she would drop him.

"Perhaps I can walk," said Flash, feeling his trousers begin to split.

And he found he could. He was dizzy and burned, and the sun was like a kettle of hot water being poured over his aching head. But if he put one foot in front of the other and counted all the flies he passed on the way, somehow he could manage to walk. The hardest thing was to tell which flies he had already counted and which were new arrivals. They all wanted to fly into his mouth.

"What's in the box?" asked the girl, pointing.

"A camera," said Flash. "I'm a photographer. That's what I do. Photographs."

"Ah!" said the girl. And there was something about the empty coffee swirl of her eyes that told him instantly: she had never seen either a camera or a photographer before.

Refer to the text when answering these questions

1. What sort of landscape was the plane flying over? *(1 mark)*

2. What did Flash entitle 'Scorching the Sky'? *(1 mark)*

3. How do we know Flash was flying the plane? *(2 marks)*

4. Find two phrases that the author uses to describe the girl's appearance. *(2 marks)*

5. How does the writer use ideas related to photography to describe the plane crash? *(3 marks)*

6. What impression of the girl does this extract give you? Use evidence from the text to support your answer. *(3 marks)*

HOW DID YOU DO?

See page 64 for an example answer.

Ten things found in a wizard's pocket

A dark night.
Some words that nobody could ever spell.
A glass of water, full to the top.
A large elephant.
A vest made from spider's webs.
A handkerchief the size of a car park.
A bill from the wand shop.
A bucket full of stars and planets, to mix with the dark night.
A bag of magic mints you can suck for ever.
A snoring rabbit.

Ian McMillan

Counting the stars

It's late at night
and John is counting the stars
He's walking through the woods
and counting the stars.
The night is clear
and the stars are like salt
on a black table cloth.
John counts silently,
his lips moving, his head tilted.
It's late at night
and John is counting the stars
until he walks into a tree
that he never saw
because he was counting the stars.
Look at John
lying in the woods.
The woodland creatures are gathering around him
laughing.
in little woodland voices.
MORAL: Even when you're looking up,
Don't forget to look down.

Ian McMillan

Practice questions

1. Which animals would you find in the wizard's pocket? *(1 mark)*

2. What do you think the wizard had just bought? *(1 mark)*

3. Choose one of the objects found in the wizard's pocket and explain how and why the wizard might use it. *(3 marks)*

4. In the 'Counting the stars' poem, how does the author describe the stars? *(1 mark)*

5. Explain the moral of the poem 'Counting the stars' in your own words. *(2 marks)*

6. Did you like the 'Counting the stars' poem? (Yes/No) Give your reasons. *(3 marks)*

HOW DID YOU DO?
See page 64 for an example answer.

HANDWRITING

Achieved?

Handwriting is assessed in the Long Writing Task, so do your best to keep it neat and easy to read. You can get a maximum of three marks for handwriting, and if you follow these hints and examples, they will be easy points to achieve!

The Golden Rules

- Space out words and sentences evenly.
- Write on the lines if you are using lined paper.
- Use a pen or pencil that you feel comfortable with and always use an eraser to rub out mistakes.
- Keep the letters the same size.

Example: 1 mark handwriting

Once upon a time, long ago there was a princess. She was the most beutiful princess in the world. Her dress sparkled as much as her charming attitude. She was the happiest prettiest person in the world.

If your handwriting looks like this, you need to work on:
- Joining up letters so they flow together neatly.
- Keeping the letters the same size.
- Spacing out the letters evenly. Some of these words are quite squashed!

Example: 2 mark handwriting

Once upon a time, long ago there was a princess. She was the most beautiful princess in all the land. Her dress Sparkled as much as her charming attitude. She was the happiest, prettiest person in the world.

If your handwriting looks like this, you need to work on:
- Making sure all, not just some, of the letters are joined together.
- Getting the ascenders (the upward parts of letters like d and b) to face the same direction.

Overall, the shape and size of the letters are even and the writing is easy to read.

Example: 3 mark handwriting

Once upon a time, long ago there was a princess. She was the most beautiful princess in all the land. Her dress sparkled as much as her charming attitude. She was the happiest, prettiest person in the world.

If your handwriting looks like this, you're going to get top marks! The letters are all correctly formed and are evenly sized and spaced. The other good thing about this handwriting is that it has its own style, so try to develop a style of your own.

★ Hints and Tips

- Compare a sample of your handwriting with the ones on this page. Which one is it most like? What are you doing well? What do you need to work on to make it better?
- Go over what needs improving with a highlighter pen, then rewrite the same sample, making as many improvements as you can.
- Practise a few sentences at a time, rewriting them and making improvements.
- Try especially hard to join the letters – it really speeds up writing!

ANSWERS

Page 15

Getting dressed

What you need
- Pants
- Socks
- T shirt
- Trousers
- Sweatshirt
- Trainers

What you do

First put on the pants. These are small and white with three holes in them. Put your legs through the two smaller holes.

Next put on the socks. There are two of these. They are long, grey tubes. Put one on each foot.

Then put on the T shirt. It goes over your head and has two holes for your arms.

Put on the trousers. These are also grey but are much bigger than the socks. They go over the pants and socks.

Now put on the sweatshirt over the T shirt. It is blue and has a badge on the front.

Finally put on the trainers. These are white and go on each foot. You will need to fasten the Velcro strips.

Now you will look just like all the other pupils – apart from your green hair.

Page 17

Hi kids!

Hope all is well back there on planet Earth.

This is a really interesting planet that we are on at the mo. There's no atmosphere so of course we have to wear spacesuits the whole time. As you know I really love living in my suit – not! And it's completely flat – not a hill in sight.

The aliens are pretty friendly. They all look exactly the same so it's very difficult to tell who's who. They are about the size of a five year old child and have two rather large antennae on their heads. They use these to taste, smell and hear with.

Most of the aliens work on the land. But they're certainly not farmers as we know them. They 'grow' all their own communication equipment. So, wherever you look there are fields of what look like mini mobile phone aerials. At least it means that there is no problem with contacting you two!

Anyway, will write again soon.

All my love

Dad

Page 19

Dear Miss Smith

I'm sorry that Wayne has not got his football kit with him today. I would like to explain why this has happened.

Last night I washed his kit but did not realise that a pair of his sister's red pants were also in the machine. These pants caused the white shorts and shirt to turn pink. Wayne said that he would certainly not wear pink kit so I washed them again. This time I added bleach so that the pink colour would come out. As a result, the kit turned white again.

Then I tumble dried the kit and placed them neatly in the washing basket. This morning I discovered that the cat had brought in three dead mice and placed them on the shirt and shorts in the washing basket. Unfortunately, these mice caused a terrible mess due to the state they were in.

In order to make Wayne's kit hygienic enough to wear, I have washed it again. It was not dry when he came to school so that is why he doesn't have it with him.

I will make sure that it is ready for tomorrow.

With best wishes

Mrs Rooney

Page 21

Christmas Fair.

When? Saturday 1st December 2.30 – 4.30pm
Where? Hillview School hall
Come and meet Santa – free presents for all under 5s
Fantastic raffle prizes. Terrific tombola.
Mince pies and carols around the tree
We look forward to seeing you there!

ANSWERS

Page 23

Did he fall?
- Eggs are not the right shape to sit on walls.
- Humpty was seen wobbling before the event by one of the King's men.
- He might have been frightened by the King's horses.
- He may have slipped when he was trying to climb down the ladder.
- Two rungs were missing from the ladder.

Was he pushed?
- Goldilocks was seen in the vicinity by one of the King's men.
- She has been in trouble before.
- She did not like eggs – she would only eat porridge.
- Goldilocks has been heard teasing Humpty about his shape.
- Two blonde hairs were found at the scene of the crime.

Page 42

a) The day began well until it started to pour down with torrential rain.
b) The blossom makes the garden look beautiful although it only lasts for a couple of weeks.
c) My sister's room is a mess, because she never takes the time to tidy it up.
d) The ravenous lion continued to eat, despite the fact it had been eating for over an hour.

Page 43

a) Sam thought that London was a very noisy city.
b) Where was that cat?
c) It was a windy Monday in March when Kylie first met Jack.

Page 44

1) The dog's feet had been dried, but it still managed to tread soil onto the carpet.
2) Even though they were excited, the children were very well behaved at the carnival.
3) Looking down into the bath water, she could see that the glitter had risen to the surface and was stuck to her legs.
4) Until she was old enough, my younger sister was not allowed to go out by herself.

Page 45

1)

I'm	I am
isn't	is not
couldn't	could not
don't	do not
he's	he is
they've	they have
we'll	we will

2)

has not	hasn't
did not	didn't
you are	you're
I would	I'd
we have	we've
it is	it's
we are	we're

Page 46

1) The man's bicycle stood against the wall.
2) The cow's horn had to be cut short.
3) The girl's shoes were too tight.
4) The boys' pencils were the same.
5) The dog's tail wagged happily at his owner.
6) The dragons' talons scratched at each other's faces.
7) The child's book was torn in two.
8) Volcanoes' lava can travel at terrific speeds.
9) A river's journey comes to its end at the sea.
10) Trees' branches swayed and rustled as the storm approached.

Page 46

Suddenly a strange, gnarled little man appeared from nowhere. He had a long, white beard filled with seaweed and boots made from sea shells.

"Who are you?" gasped the fisherman, his eyes widening.

The tiny man jumped up onto the boat. "You must be handsomely rewarded," he said to the fisherman.

Page 49

1) foxes, roads, bunches, wishes, sounds, lives, taxes, trees, drinks, pirates, houses, donkeys, flies, buses

Page 50

Short vowel sounds
bin, chat, flutter, wet, light, dot

Long vowel sounds
line, paper, choose, reign, meet, float

Page 51

Verb	Past tense	Present tense	Future tense
To fit	I have fitted, I fitted, I was fitting	I fit, I am fitting	I will fit
To move	I have moved, I moved, I was moving	I move, I am moving	I will move
To bite	I have bitten, I bit, I was biting	I bite, I am biting	I will bite
To clap	I have clapped, I clapped, I was clapping	I clap, I am clapping	I will clap
To keep	I have kept, I kept, I was keeping	I keep, I am keeping	I will keep
To swim	I have swum, I swam, I was swimming	I swim, I am swimming	I will swim
To light	I have lit, I lit, I was lighting	I light, I am lighting	I will light
To fly	I have flown, I flew, I was flying	I fly, I am flying	I will fly
To injure	I have injured, I injured, I was injuring	I injure, I am injuring	I will injure
To watch	I have watched, I watched, I was watching	I watch, I am watching	I will watch
To produce	I have produced, I produced, I was producing	I produce, I am producing	I will produce
To dance	I have danced, I danced, I was dancing	I dance, I am dancing	I will dance
To try	I have tried, I tried, I was trying	I try, I am trying	I will try
To pursue	I have pursued, I pursued, I was pursuing	I pursue, I am pursuing	I will pursue
To cheat	I have cheated, I cheated, I was cheating	I cheat, I am cheating	I will cheat

Page 52

Spelling Test

Section A
1) crunches
2) aunts
3) taxes
4) hippies
5) werewolves
6) lunches
7) ponies
8) chairs
9) sofas
10) hippopotami/hippopotamuses

Section B

'ing
1) batting
2) trotting
3) shooting
4) weeping
5) sleeping

'ed
1) snorted
2) looked
3) mapped
4) slapped
5) shopped

'er
1) stronger
2) louder
3) bigger
4) redder
5) softer

Section C
1) I braked
2) I will grow
3) I sharpened
4) I skip
5) stripes
6) actress
7) known
8) perfectly
9) thieves
10) reigned

Section D

Correct spellings as follows:

Dinosaurs, atmosphere, survived
extinct, creatures, successful
exactly, conditions, existed
scientists, insects, probably
giant, adaptable, current

Page 57

1) 3 metres
2) Flores dragons are red and yellow, komodo dragons are greyish brown.
3) Komodo, Rinca and Flores
4) Any example from the text.
5) Reference to saliva, bacteria and blood poisoning.
6) Reference to specific actions compared to human wrestlers.
7) Ideas to combat hunting, loss of prey species and habitat loss.
8) Reference to appearance, feeding habits and rarity.

Page 59

1) desert, gulches, valleys and lakes.
2) The image of the burning plane.
3) 'He was all alone in the plane' quoted from the text. (1 mark for answer that includes reference to being in the cockpit)
4) Any two phrases from the text.
5) Reference to pictures, frames, focus, cinema films, camera shutters, darkroom, etc.
6) Can speak English, is practical, is a leader, intelligent, inquisitive, poor.
(1 mark if only descriptions of her appearance are given)

Page 61

1) elephant, rabbit
2) A wand
3) Answers will vary.
4) 'like salt on a black table cloth'
5) Answers will vary.
6) Answers will vary.